Mystics at Prayer
▽ ▽ ▽

Mystics at Prayer

▽

Compiled by

FR. MANY CIHLAR, F.R.C.
VIENNA, AUSTRIA

With Introduction by

DR. H. SPENCER LEWIS, F.R.C.

ROSICRUCIAN LIBRARY

VOLUME IX

SUPREME GRAND LODGE OF AMORC

Printing and Publishing Department

San Jose, California

First Edition, March, 1931

Supreme Grand Lodge of AMORC, Inc.
All Rights Reserved

Library of Congress Catalog Card No.: 36-17108

ISBN 0-912057-08-4

Nineteenth Edition, 1982
Second Printing, 1984

COMPILER'S DEDICATION

———

I dedicate this book with the deepest
and most respectful esteem
to
(Mrs.) Gladys R. Lewis,
wife of the Imperator of
A M O R C

THE ROSICRUCIAN LIBRARY
·   ·   ·
· ·   · ··

(Other volumes will be added from time to time.
Write for complete catalogue.)

PREFACE

.· .· .·

This unique book contains a carefully selected group of prayers found in the personal and private writings of many well-known characters and in the liturgy of various religious movements.

They have been selected by Mr. Cihlar after a careful study of the prayers of all peoples and all nations in relation to the processes of mystical attunement and spiritual development.

Mr. Cihlar is a Rosicrucian, a high officer in this time-honored and beautiful body of Mystics, adhering to and promulgating the divine principles of earthly life.

From his sanctum in Vienna, Austria, his manuscript was sent to America that it might be published by the Western World branch of the Rosicrucian Order and given to the people of this new world with the hope that it may lead to a greater desire to pray and a greater efficiency in the manner of praying.

We trust that this hope will be fulfilled by the widespread distribution of this book and the daily reference to the prayers contained in it.

THE PUBLISHERS

INTRODUCTION

▽

HOW TO PRAY

An examination of the prayers which appear on the following pages reveals the fact that the great mystics of all ages understood the real processes of prayer and knew how to pray.

Christians have the beautiful example of the prayer given to them by Jesus, the Christ, as a standard; and it is a most beautiful standard. But, long before the Christian era, the Mystics, the Avatars, and those through whom the Light of God shone among men, knew by divine inspiration how to pray. Examples of their prayers contained in these pages prove this fact.

The Mystic and those who were touched with the Light of Cosmic Consciousness had a very definite understanding of the processes of prayer. In the Western World today millions of persons have digressed very greatly from these processes, and, making their prayers long and filled with personal petitions, are often disappointed with the seeming lack of efficacy in their prayers or the inefficacy of praying. It may be permissible, therefore, briefly to outline or review true processes of prayer as understood by the Mystics.

According to the mystical viewpoint, praying to God is based upon the conviction that God is omnipotent in power, present everywhere, and willing to listen to our sincere petitions. This is all that we should have in mind when praying. The average person in praying, however, has in mind some assumptions which mislead him in wording his prayers, and in approaching the very attitude of prayer. He assumes that God is not only omnipotent in power, omnipresent, and merciful, but that with all of His power, with all of His intelligence, with all of His mastership and control throughout the world, and with all

His attunement with the beings which He created, **He is, nevertheless, ignorant of our wants and needs, and completely unacquainted with what we require in life in order to live abundantly and secure our everyday necessities.** Very often, the prayerful petitioner also assumes that God has given no thought to the outcome of certain contests in life or struggles between various factions of human beings, and is incapable of justly deciding such contests or awarding the victory to the right side. These false assumptions are responsible for the mistakes that are made in prayer and for the failure of prayers to be highly efficacious.

To go into prayer with the idea or belief that God does not know what we need or even what we want, or what is best for us, and that we must advise Him, argue with Him, stress our viewpoint and convince Him, **or at least urge Him,** to adopt our ideas and decisions and grant what we plead for, is to make the most serious mistake in the process of praying.

In the first place, the process of prayer is a transcendent method of **communion with God.** It is the most intimate, personal contact that human beings can make with their Father, the Creator of all beings. This sublime period of communion should be approached with clean thoughts, but most of all with a clear understanding of our privileges and a total absence of any feeling that we have any **right** to petition God to grant our wishes.

The Mystics know, also, that true prayer is based upon a Cosmic and Spiritual law. That law is this: "Seek and ye shall find, knock and it shall be opened unto you." The ancient mystical injunction was that you must **ask** in order to receive, that you must proffer your hand in order to have the token given unto you, that you must **express** your desire before it will be answered. In all mystical processes, the expression of a sincere wish or desire, opens wide the doorway to the reception of spiritual blessings. The asking in sincerity and the reverential expression of such wishes attunes the person with the one who has the power to give and, unless there is a meeting of the minds and a meeting of the consciousness of both persons, there can neither be attunement nor the passing from one to the other of the spiritual things desired. To the Mystic, therefore, prayer is a meeting of the minds. It is not an occasion for personal petitioning, but for **spiritual communion.** It is a time when the soul within us and the deepest and most inner parts of our being sacredly, sincerely, and quietly speak to God and express the deepest wishes of our hearts and minds. The belief, therefore, that our human conception of our needs must be outlined in minutest detail and expressed in great elaboration is also a misconception, since the thoughts moving us to prayer are easily transmitted to the divine consciousness during this communion, and the lips need only speak the fewest words of appreciation and thankfulness.

Prayers should not consist of a categorical representation of details or a long list of the things that we feel we want, but merely an expression of a desire for divine blessings. Have we any right to come before God in this privileged period of communion and demand, or even plead, that long life be given to us because we desire it and have come to the conclusion that it is the thing we should have? Is that not an indication that we have concluded that God may not have thought about our lives or may have ordained otherwise, or differently, and that we hope to change His mind or set aside His wise decrees because of our petition? Have we any right to come before the Creator of all, and say that we **want** this, that, or the other thing in a manner which intimates that we have outlined and decided upon such things as being **our judgment** of what is best for us?

If we lived in a great kingdom under a most just and merciful king, and were enjoying every benediction and blessing that the king could bestow upon the multitudes

who lived under him, and we were notified that we had
the **extraordinary privilege** of coming before this king in
personal communion, and during this communion we
might express our great desires in some form of prayerful
petition, would we not hesitate for a long time in formu-
lating our desires and arranging the expressions we would
use? Undoubtedly, when the moment came to face the
king and be permitted to open our lips and speak any
words at all, we would first utter some words of profound thankfulness for the blessings we had enjoyed,
and humbly add that **if it pleased the king,** we would be
happy to continue enjoying the same blessings or possibly
a few more. Not one of us would think of attempting
to petition this king to grant us a long list of material
things, nor ask him to give us victory over others, or to
make any exception in the universal standard of living,
that we might rise above all our fellow men in the kingdom; nor would we ask for many of the things that
were most desired. We would be so happy in the fact
that the king had granted us the privilege of communion
that we would be moved to an attitude of thankfulness
and an expression of appreciation for what we had, rather
than entering into a demand for many other things.

How many go into prayer or come before the consciousness of God in Holy Communion in this attitude?
How many cleanse their hands of debt by first thanking
God for each individual blessing throughout the day?
How many approach God in prayer in an attitude of
profound appreciation for the very life and consciousness
which animates their beings? After all, is not the gift
of life the greatest blessing that God can give, and if
we have it, have we not that which is greater than
anything else we may desire? To ask for other things
than life or to petition for anything other than the
consciousness of God in our beings is to lift lesser things
and insignificant things above the greatest.

From the mystical point of view, our prayers should be
expressions of desires for a continuation of the bene-

dictions God has already granted, and which He, in His supreme wisdom, has seen fit to bestow upon us. Ever uppermost in our minds should be the thought that, "Thy will, not mine be done." The simple expression of, "May it please the Father of us all that health may return to my body," is a more concise, honest, and worthy petition than one that demands or suggests that God change the law now in operation in our bodies, and set aside certain specific conditions and establish others, simply because this is the conclusion that we have reached, and is our greatest desire at the moment. A prayer for victory should not be asked by the vainglorious one who has reached the conclusion that he, above all others, should be the victorious one in a contest, and that God has made no decision and is waiting for man to present his conclusion.

By examining the prayers we will find that the Mystics always assumed that whatever might be their lot in life, and however the state of their health or the condition of the circumstances surrounding them, be they ill or fortunate, all things proceeded from God and were ordained by Him and, therefore, were just and in accordance with some law or some principle, merciful, and necessary to human experience. The fact that man in his finite and undeveloped understanding could not comprehend the reason for these experiences, or believe them to be wrong, unnecessary, or undesirable, does not warrant man in coming before God in the Holy Communion of prayer with the conclusion that his finite and undeveloped understanding is correct, and that God is in error or in ignorance of the conditions and needs to be advised and petitioned to make certain changes or to recall or undo His decrees.

As we shall see in the following pages the Mystics approached God with the attitude that whatever was their lot in life would be gladly and silently accepted, and all pains and suffering endured, **if it be the will of**

God. We find in many of these prayers the thought expressed that even the sufferings and trials, and the tribulations in life, were appreciated since they were unquestionably the result of God's plan being worked out in the individual for some ultimate purpose unquestionably good and profitable.

The fact that we are not surrounded by any restrictions in regard to prayer and that God has given us the consciousness and ability, as well as the privilege, of approaching Him in Holy Communion and of attuning ourselves with Him at any hour of the day or any moment in our lives, is in itself a divine gift or concession that the Mystics valued above all things. Therefore, prayer was approached with thankfulness in every sense, and the first expression uttered by the lips was words of appreciation and thanks.

Learn **how to pray,** and make prayer the real pleasure of your life, for it brings you in closer contact with the great Ruler of the universe than you can ever approach Him while living on this earthly plane of existence. Make your Holy Communions frequent. Thank God for the breath of life and the return of consciousness when you arise in the morning. Silently thank Him for every morsel of food at mealtime. Express your appreciation for every pleasure, every worldly gift, every moment of happiness, and every rich reward of your efforts or the efforts of others. At the close of day, enter into Holy Communion of prayer and express your faith and trust in His divine guidance of your soul and consciousness throughout the night, and again be thankful for the day and al! the opportunities it contained to carry out your desires and ambitions, and to enjoy the divine blessings. Make prayer the transcendental and sublime pleasure of your inner self—more important, more enjoyable, more uplifting and benefiting to your entire being than any other of your earthly experiences.

You will find many of the prayers on the following pages useful either in their precise wording, or as a guide and help in learning how to express the thoughts of your soul. The more you pray in the proper attitude, the more spiritually attuned you will become, and the richer will be the influx of the blessings from the Cosmic through the great love and mercy of God.

H. SPENCER LEWIS, F.R.C.

Temple of Alden
Rosicrucian Park
San Jose, California.

**The Book
of the Dead**

O THOTH, let, I pray, THY face be towards me. Make THOU my word to be Maat* against my enemies, as THOU didst make the word of Osiris to be Maat against his enemies.

∴ ∴ ∴

**A
Babylonian
Prayer**

O LORD, do not cast THY servant off!
In the deep watery morass he lies—take hold of his hand!
The sin that I have committed, change to grace!
The transgressions that I have committed, let the wind carry off!

∴ ∴ ∴

**Psalm
19:14**

Let the words of my mouth and the meditation of my heart be acceptable in THY sight, O LORD, my strength and my redeemer.

∴ ∴ ∴

**Syrian
Clementine
Liturgy**

O GOD, WHO art the unsearchable abyss of peace, the ineffable sea of love, the fountain of blessings and the bestower of affection, Who sendest peace to those that receive it. Open to us the sea of THY love and water us with the plenteous streams from the riches of THY grace. Make us children of quietness and heirs of peace. Enkindle in us the fire of THY love; sow in us THY fear; strengthen our weakness by THY power; and bind us closely to THEE and to each in one firm bond of unity.

* Maat is the Egyptian word for truth.

Prayer of Manasses

O LORD ALMIGHTY, which art in heaven,
THOU GOD of our fathers,
Of Abraham and Isaac and Jacob
And of their righteous seed;
THOU who hast made the heaven and the earth,
With all the array thereof,
Who hast bound the sea by the word of THY command;
Who hast shut up the Deep, and sealed it
With THY terrible and glorious Name.
Infinite and unsearchable in THY merciful promise.
For THOU art the LORD MOST HIGH, of great compassion, long-suffering and abundant in mercy, and repentest THEE for the evils of men.
THOU, O LORD, according to THY great goodness hast promised repentance and forgiveness to them that have sinned against THEE, and in the multitude of THY mercies hast appointed repentance unto sinners, that they may be saved.

∴   ∴   ∴

Pericles

Grant that no word may fall from me against my will unfit for the present need.

∴   ∴   ∴

Emperor Julian

Point me the way that leadeth upward to THEE. For yonder regions where THOU dwellest are incomparably beautiful, if I may divine their beauty that is at THY side from the pleasantness of the Path which I have already traveled.

Zoroaster

With bended knees, with hand out-
stretched, I pray to THEE, my LORD,
O INVISIBLE BENEVOLENT SPIRIT!
Vouchsafe to me in this hour of joy,
All righteousness of action, all wisdom
of the good mind,
That I may thereby bring joy to the
Soul of Creation.

∴   ∴   ∴

Zoroaster

All that I ought to have thought and
have not thought;
All that I ought to have said and have
not said;
All that I ought to have done and have
not done;
All that I ought not to have thought and
yet have thought;
All that I ought not to have spoken and
yet have spoken;
All that I ought not to have done and
yet have done;
For thoughts, words and works, pray I for
forgiveness, and repent of with penance.

∴   ∴   ∴

Socrates

Grant me to be beautiful within, and
all I have of outward things to be at
peace with those within.

∴   ∴   ∴

**Jacobite
Liturgy**

O GOD, the FATHER, ORIGIN of
DIVINITY, GOOD beyond all that is good,
FAIR beyond all that is fair, in WHOM is
calmness, peace and concord; bring us all
back into an unity of love, which may bear
some likeness to THY sublime nature.

Jesus Christ	Our FATHER, WHO art in heaven, hallowed be THY name, THY kingdom come, THY will be done on earth as it is done in heaven. Give us this day our daily bread, and forgive us our trespasses as we ought to forgive those that trespass against us. Lead us when in temptation, but deliver us from evil. Amen.

.'. .'. .'.

Liturgy of the Greek Church	That which we know not, do THOU reveal; that which is wanting in us do THOU fill up; in that which we know, do THOU strengthen us.

.'. .'. .'.

Liturgy of St. Mark	We give THEE thanks—yea, more than thanks—O LORD our GOD, for all THY goodness at all times and in all places.

.'. .'. .'.

St. Ephrem the Syrian	THOU hast quieted those which were in confusion. Praise to THY calmness, praise to THY reconciliation, O LORD GOD.

.'. .'. .'.

St. Chrysostom	Thanks be to THEE, O GOD, for everything.

.'. .'. .'.

St. Basil	Steer THOU the vessel of our life towards THYSELF, THOU tranquil Haven of all storm-tossed souls. Show us the course wherein we should go.

**St. Chry-
sostom**

Into THY guidance and care, O LORD,
THOU LOVER of Man, we entrust all our
life and hope.

∴   ∴   ∴

St. Patrick

May the Strength of GOD pilot us. May
the Power of GOD preserve us. May the
Wisdom of GOD instruct us. May the
Way of GOD direct us.

∴   ∴   ∴

Synesius

O UNITY, THEE I sing by voices or by
silence; for both are alike significant to
THEE.

∴   ∴   ∴

St. Blasius

May GOD, the uncreated ABYSS, vouchsafe to call unto HIMSELF our Spirit, the
created abyss, and make it one with HIM,
that our spirit, plunged in the deep sea
of the GODHEAD, may happily lose itself
in the Spirit of GOD.

∴   ∴   ∴

Synesius

I hymn THEE, O BLESSED ONE, by
means of voice, and I hymn THEE, O
BLESSED ONE, by means of silence; for
THOU perceivest as much from silence
spiritual as from voice.

∴   ∴   ∴

**Sarum
Breviary**

ALMIGHTY GOD, we invoke THEE,
the fountain of everlasting Light, and
entreat THEE to send forth THY truth into
our hearts, and to pour upon us the glory
of THY Brightness.

Synesius

Behold THY suppliant attempting to mount; enlighten me, enable my wings, relax my fetters. May I escape from the body to THY bosom whence flows the Soul's source. Restore me to the Spring whence I was poured forth. Grant that beneath the ordering of my SIRE, I may sing in union with the ROYAL CHOIR. Let me mingle with the Light, and never more sink to earth.

∴   ∴   ∴

Gelasian Sacramentary

O GOD of unchangeable Power, let the whole world feel and see that things which were cast down are being raised up, that those which had grown old are being made new and that all things are returning to perfection.

∴   ∴   ∴

Leonine Sacramentary

Grant us, O LORD, not to mind earthly things, but to love things heavenly; and even now while we are placed among things that are passing away, to cleave to those that shall abide.

∴   ∴   ∴

Mohammed

O LORD, grant us to love THEE; grant that we may love those that love THEE; grant that we may do the deeds that win THY love. Make the love of THEE to be dearer than ourselves, our families, than wealth, and even than cool water.

∴   ∴   ∴

St. Augustine

Come LORD and work. Arouse us and incite. Kindle us, sweep us onwards. Be fragrant as flowers, sweet as honey. Teach us to love and to run.

St. Augustine

Grant us to know THEE and love THEE and, rejoice in THEE. And if we cannot do these perfectly in this life, let us at least advance to higher degrees every day till we can come to do them to perfection.

.: .: .:

St. Augustine

LORD, teach me to know THEE, and to know myself.

.: .: .:

St. Augustine

We seek THY face, turn THY face unto us, and show us THY glory. Then shall our longing be satisfied, and our peace shall be perfect.

.: .: .:

St. Augustine

LORD, when I look upon mine own life it seems THOU hast led me so carefully, so tenderly, THOU canst have attended to none else; but when I see how wonderfully THOU hast led the world and art leading it, I am amazed that THOU hast had time to attend to such as I.

.: .: .:

St. Augustine

Take THOU possession of us. We give our whole selves to THEE, make known to us what THOU requirest of us, and we will accomplish it.

.: .: .:

St. Augustine

O GOD, where was I wandering to seek THEE? O most infinite Beauty, I sought THEE without, and THOU wast in the midst of my heart.

St. Augustine

O GOD, WHO dost grant us what we ask, if only when we ask we live a better life.

∴ ∴ ∴

Coptic Apocrypha

Glory be to THEE, PROPITIATOR.
Glory be to THEE, UNDYING ONE.
Glory be to THEE, KING of PEACE.
Glory be to THEE, WHO was not born.
Glory be to THEE, the INCORRUPTIBLE.
Glory be to THEE, KING of GLORY.
Glory be to THEE, the HEAD of the UNIVERSE.
Glory be to THEE, HOLY and PERFECT ONE.
Glory be to THEE, THOU TREASURY of GLORY.
Glory be to THEE, THOU true Light.
Glory be to THEE, DELIVERER of the UNIVERSE.
Glory be to THEE, THOU WHO art indeed the GOOD ONE.
Glory be to THEE, ALPHA of the UNIVERSE.
Glory be to THEE, LIFE of the UNIVERSE.
O SWEET NAME.
O THOU, WHO art at the head of the Universe.
O THOU Beginning and End of everything. Amen.

∴ ∴ ∴

St. Anselm

O THOU plenteous Source of every good and perfect gift, shed abroad the cheering light of THY sevenfold grace over our hearts.

**Collect
from the
sixth
Century**

O GOD who hast folded back the man-
tle of the night to clothe us in the glory of
the day, chase from our hearts all gloomy
thoughts, and make us glad with the
brightness of hope that we may effectively
aspire to unknown virtues.

∴ ∴ ∴

Alcuin

O ETERNAL LIGHT, shine into our
hearts. O ETERNAL GOODNESS, deliver
us from evil. O ETERNAL POWER, be
THOU our support. ETERNAL WISDOM,
scatter the darkness of our ignorance.
ETERNAL PITY, have mercy upon us.

∴ ∴ ∴

**John Scotus
Erigena**

O THOU, WHO art the everlasting
essence of things beyond space and time
and yet within them; THOU WHO tran-
scendest yet pervadest all things; manifest
THYSELF to us, feeling after THEE, seeking THEE in the shades of ignorance, yet
seeking nothing beside THEE.

∴ ∴ ∴

St. Anselm

Pierce with the arrows of THY love the
secret chambers of the inner man. Let the
entrance of THY healthful flames set the
sluggish heart alight; and the burning fire
of THY sacred inspiration enlighten it.

∴ ∴ ∴

**St. Hilde-
gard**

OMNIPOTENT FATHER, out of THEE
flows a fountain in fiery heat; lead THY
sons by a favourable wind through the
mystic waters.

St. Bernard

I love THEE because I love; I love that I may love.

.˙. .˙. .˙.

St. Bernard

In what blaze of Glory dost THOU rise, O SUN OF RIGHTEOUSNESS, from the heart of the earth, after THY setting!

In what resplendent Vesture, O KING of GLORY, dost THOU enter again the highest heaven!

At the sight of all these marvels, how can I do otherwise than cry: "All my bones shall say, 'LORD, who is like unto THEE?' "

.˙. .˙. .˙.

St. Bernard

If THOU, LORD, art so good to those who seek, what shall THY goodness be to those who find?

.˙. .˙. .˙.

St. Thomas Aquinas

Give me, O LORD, a steadfast heart, which no unworthy affection may drag downwards; give me an unconquered heart, which no tribulation can wear out; give me an upright heart, which no unworthy purpose may tempt aside.

Bestow upon me also, O LORD, my GOD, understanding to know THEE, diligence to seek THEE, wisdom to find THEE, and a faithfulness that may finally embrace THEE.

.˙. .˙. .˙.

St. Thomas Aquinas

Grant me fervently to desire, wisely to search out, and perfectly to fulfill all that is well-pleasing unto THEE.

St. Richard

May we know THEE more clearly, love THEE more dearly, and follow THEE more nearly.

∴ ∴ ∴

Dame Gertrude More

O my GOD, let me walk in the way of love which knoweth not how to seek self in anything whatsoever. Let this love wholly possess my soul and heart, which, I beseech THEE may live and move only in, and out of, a pure and sincere love to THEE. Let me love THEE for THYSELF, and nothing else but in THEE and for THEE. Let me love nothing instead of THEE; for to give all for love is a most sweet bargain.

∴ ∴ ∴

Ali Bin Uthman

THY will be done, O my LORD and MASTER.
O THOU who art my Spirit's treasure MEANING.
O ESSENCE of my being, O GOAL of my desire,
O my SPEECH and HINTS and my GESTURES.
O all of my all, O my HEARING and my SIGHT.
O my WHOLE and my ELEMENT and my PARTICLES.

∴ ∴ ∴

Mozarabic Liturgy

Do THOU meet us while we walk in the Way and long to reach the Country; so that following THY light we may keep the Way of righteousness and never wander away into the darkness of this world's night.

Jalal-ud-din Rumi

O THOU who art my Soul's comfort in the season of sorrow,
O THOU who art my Spirit's treasure in the bitterness of death,
That which the imagination hath not conceived;
That which the understanding hath not seen;
Visited my Soul from THEE.
Hence, in worship, I turn towards THEE.

∴ ∴ ∴

Jalal-ud-din Rumi

O GOD, THY grace is the proper object of our desire;
To couple others with THEE is not proper.
Nothing is bitterer than severance from THEE,
Without THY shelter there is naught but perplexity.
Our worldly goods rob us of our heavenly goods,
Our body rends the garment of our soul.
Our hands, as it were, prey on our feet;
Without reliance on THEE how can we live?
And if the soul escapes these great perils,
It is made captive as a victim of misfortunes and fears
Inasmuch as when the soul lacks union with the Beloved,
It abides for ever blind and darkened by itself.

Dante

Give us this day the daily manna, without which through this rough desert he backward goes who toils most to go on.

.∙. .∙. .∙.

Sufi Invocation

Praise be to THEE, O HIDDEN ONE and MANIFESTED ONE. Praise be to THY Glory, to THY Might, to THY Power, and to THY Great Skill.

O ALLAH, to THEE all greatness belongs. O THOU who possessest the Power and Beauty and Perfection. THOU art the Spirit of All.

Praise to THEE, O SOVEREIGN of all Monarchs; to THEE, O MASTER of all affairs; to THEE, O CONTROLLER of all things; to THEE, RULER of all BEINGS.

THOU art free from death, free from birth and free from all limitations. O THOU ETERNAL ONE, THOU art free from all conditions, pure from all things. O ALLAH, THOU art the GOD of Souls on earth; THOU art the LORD of Hosts in the Heavens.

.∙. .∙. .∙.

Ruysbroeck

O LORD, I gasp in my desire for THEE, yet can I not consume THEE. The more I eat—the fiercer is my hunger; the more I drink—the greater is my thirst. I follow after that which flieth from me, and as I follow, my desire groweth greater.

.∙. .∙. .∙.

Ruysbroeck

O LORD, THOU desirest my spirit in the inward parts, that I may see THEE as THOU seest me, and love THEE as THOU lovest me.

Tauler

As the sun-flower ever turning
   To the mighty sun,
With the faithfulness of fealty
   Following only one—
     So make me, LORD, to THEE.

         ∴ ∴ ∴

Tauler

We honour and glorify THY unspeakable
mystery with holy reverence and silence.

         ∴ ∴ ∴

Angela of Foligno

O SUPREME GOOD, THOU hast de-
signed to make us know that THOU art
Love, and makest us in love with that love;
wherefore they who come before THY face
shall be rewarded according unto their
love, and there is nothing which leadeth
the contemplative unto contemplation sav-
ing true love alone.

         ∴ ∴ ∴

Suso

THOU hast granted my heart's desire—
   Most blest of the blessed is he
Who findeth no rest and no sweetness
   Till he rests, O LORD, in THEE.

         ∴ ∴ ∴

Suso

It is meet that I should be enamoured
of THEE, and whatever I shall know to be
THY dearest will that I will always do.

         ∴ ∴ ∴

Suso

Gentle LORD, cause some sweet fruit
of good instruction to issue forth from our
sharp thorns of sufferings, that we may
suffer more patiently, and be better able
to offer up our sufferings to THY praise
and glory.

Andrewes

Unto all men everywhere give THY grace and THY blessing.

.· .· .·

St. Catherine of Siena

O LORD, I pray for all those whom THOU hast given me, whom I love with a special love and whom THOU hast made one thing with me. For they are my consolation and for THY sake I desire to see them running in the sweet and narrow way dead to self and pure from all judgment and murmuring against their neighbour. May they all attain to THEE, O ETERNAL FATHER, to THEE who art their final end.

.· .· .·

St. Catherine of Siena

Punish me for my sins in this finite Life.

.· .· .·

St. Bernardine

O GOD, acknowledge what is THINE in us, and take away from us all that is not THINE, for THY honour and glory.

.· .· .·

Lady Julian of Norwich

GOD, of THY Goodness, give me THYSELF, for THOU art enough to me, and may I nothing ask that is less, that may be full worship to THEE; and if I ask anything that is less, ever me wanteth,— but only in THEE I have all.

.· .· .·

Thomas a Kempis

Praised be THY name, not mine; magnified be THY work, not mine; blessed be THY Holy Name, but to me let no part of man's praise be given.

**Thomas
a Kempis**

Grant me, O LORD, heavenly wisdom, that I may learn above all things to seek and to find THEE; above all things to relish and to love THEE; and to think of all other things as being what indeed they are, at the disposal of THY wisdom.

∴ ∴ ∴

**Thomas
a Kempis**

O LORD, THOU knowest what is the better Way, let this or that be done, as THOU shalt please. Give what THOU wilt, and how much THOU wilt, and when THOU wilt. Deal with me as THOU knowest, and as best pleaseth THEE, and is most for THY honour. Set me where THOU wilt, and deal with me in all things just as THOU wilt. I am in THY hand; turn me round and turn me back again, even as a wheel. Behold I am THY servant, prepared for all things; for I desire not to live unto myself, but unto THEE; and oh that I could do it worthy and perfectly.

∴ ∴ ∴

Savonarola

LORD, we pray not for tranquillity, nor that our tribulations may cease; we pray for THY Spirit and THY love that THOU grant us strength and grace to overcome adversity.

∴ ∴ ∴

**St. Ignatius
Loyola**

Teach us, good LORD, to serve THEE as THOU deservest; to give and not to count the cost; to fight and not to heed the wounds; to toil and not to seek for rest; to labour and not to ask for any reward, save that of knowing that we do THY will.

**Thomas
a Kempis**

O LORD, if only my will may remain right and firm towards THEE, do with me whatsoever it shall please THEE. For it cannot be anything but good whatsoever THOU shalt do with me.

If THOU willest me to be in darkness, be THOU blessed; and if THOU willest me to be in light be THOU again blessed.

If THOU vouchsafe to comfort me, be THOU blessed; and if THOU willest me to be afflicted, be THOU ever equally blessed.

∴ ∴ ∴

**The Friend
of God**

O LORD, I wish for the love of THEE to keep from all sin today. Help me this day to do all I do to THY glory and according to THY dear will, whether my nature likes it or not.

∴ ∴ ∴

**Theologica
Germanica**

I would fain be to the ETERNAL GOODNESS what his own hand is to a man.

∴ ∴ ∴

**Nicholas
de Cusa**

Restless is my heart, O LORD, because THY love hath inflamed it with such a desire that it cannot rest but in THEE alone.

∴ ∴ ∴

St. Teresa

Govern all by THY wisdom, O LORD, so that my soul may always be serving THEE as THOU dost will and not as I may choose. Let me die to myself, so that I may serve THEE; let me live to THEE, who in THYSELF art the true life.

Erasmus

Vouchsafe to bestow upon us some portion of THY heavenly Bread, day by day, that the hunger and thirst for earthly things may diminish in us continually.

∴ ∴ ∴

St. Ignatius Loyola

Take, O LORD, and receive my entire liberty, my memory, my understanding, and my whole will. All that I am, all that I have, THOU hast given me, and I give it back again to THEE to be disposed of according to THY good pleasure. Give me only THY love and THY grace; with THEE I am rich enough, nor do I ask for aught besides.

∴ ∴ ∴

St. Teresa

Do not punish me by granting that which I wish or ask, if it offend THY love which would always live in me.

∴ ∴ ∴

St. John of the Cross

O sweetest Love of GOD, too little known; he who has found THEE is at rest.
Everywhere with THEE, O my GOD. O my love, all for THEE, nothing for me.
O my GOD, how sweet to me THY presence, Who art the SOVEREIGN GOOD. O LORD, I beseech THEE, leave me not for a moment, because I know not the value of my soul.

∴ ∴ ∴

St. Francis de Sales

O GOD, how admirable is that which we see; but O GOD, how much more so is that which we cannot see.

**St. John
of the Cross**

GOD of my life! nothing can make me
   glad,
For all my gladness springs from sight
   of THEE,
And faileth me because I have
      THEE not.
If 'tis THY will, my GOD, I live forlorn,
I'll take my longings even for my
   comfort
While dwelling in this world.
When shall there dawn that most
   delicious day,
When, O my Glory, I may joy in THEE
Delivered from this body's heavy load?
Yet if my life can bring increase of
   glory
To THINE ETERNAL BEING,
In truth I do not wish that it should end.

∴   ∴   ∴

**Book of
Christian
Prayers**

O Light which does lighten every man
that cometh into the world, without whom
all is most dark darkness, by whom all
things are most splendent; Lighten our
minds, that we may only see those things
that please THEE and may be blinded to
all other things.

∴   ∴   ∴

B. Whichcote

O GOD of the spirits of all flesh,
naturalize us to Heaven and reconcile us
to all the things of that high estate, that
so we may not drudge in the world, nor
act in a slavish spirit in ways of Religion,
but that we may serve THEE with ingenuity
of mind and with freedom of spirit, as
those that are set at liberty.

**John
Norden**

We are forced, O FATHER, to seek THEE daily, and THOU offerest THYSELF daily to be found; whensoever we seek THEE we find THEE, in the house, in the fields, in the Temple, and in the highway.

∴   ∴   ∴

**Sir Thomas
Browne**

Defend me, O GOD, from myself.

∴   ∴   ∴

**Jacob
Boehme**

In THEE would we lose ourselves utterly; do in us what THOU wilt.

∴   ∴   ∴

**Jacob
Boehme**

O THOU great incomprehensible GOD. Who fillest all, be THOU indeed my heaven. Let my spirit be indeed the music and the joy of THY spirit. Do THOU make music in me and may I make harmony in the Divine Kingdom of THY joy, in the great love of GOD, in the wonders of THY glory and splendour, in the company of THY holy angelic harmonies.

∴   ∴   ∴

**Jeremy
Taylor**

Guide me, O LORD, in all the changes and varieties of the world; that in all things that shall happen, I may have an evenness and tranquillity of spirit; that my soul may be wholly resigned to THY divinest will and pleasure, never murmuring at THY gentle chastisements and fatherly correction.

∴   ∴   ∴

**Jeremy
Taylor**

THOU, O LORD, art our Defender, THOU art our Worship, and the Lifter-up of our heads.

**Richard
Baxter**

O THOU Spirit of Life, breathe upon us THY graces in us, take us by the hand and lift us from earth.

∴ ∴ ∴

N. Culverwel

O my GOD, I'll bless THEE for those eternal treasures that are in THY self, though I should never taste of them.

∴ ∴ ∴

**Thomas
Elwood**

O that mine eyes might closed be
To what concerns me not to see;
That deafness might possess mine ear
To what concerns me not to hear;
That truth my tongue might always tie
From ever speaking foolishly;
That no vain thing might ever rest,
Or be conceived within my breast;
That by each deed and word and
     thought
Glory may to God be brought!
But what are wishes? LORD, mine eye
On THEE is fixed, to THEE I cry;
Wash, LORD, and purify my heart,
And make it clean in every part.
And when 'tis clean, LORD, keep it, too,
For that is more than I can do.

∴ ∴ ∴

T. Traherne

O give me grace to see THY face and be a constant mirror of ETERNITY.

∴ ∴ ∴

**Madame
Guyon**

THY creatures wrong THEE, O THOU
     SOV'REIGN GOOD.
THOU art not lov'd because not
     understood.

Molinos

Give me leave, O LORD, to lament our blindness and ingratitude. We all live deceived, seeking the foolish world, and forsaking THEE Who art our GOD. We forsake THEE, the Fountain of Living Waters, for the foul mire of the world.

.· .· .·

Fenelon

All we ask is to die rather than live unfaithful to THEE. Give us not life, if we shall love it too well.

.· .· .·

Pascal

LORD, I give THEE all.

.· .· .·

Fenelon

Give to us, THY children, that which we ourselves know not to ask. We would have no other desire than to accomplish THY will. Teach us to pray, pray THOU in us.

.· .· .·

Fenelon

O my GOD, preserve me from the fatal slavery that men madly call liberty. With THEE alone is freedom. It is THY truth that makes us free. To serve THEE is true dominion.

.· .· .·

Fenelon

LORD, I know not what I ought to ask of THEE; THOU only knowest what I need; THOU lovest me better than I know how to love myself. O FATHER, give to THY child that which he himself knows not how to ask.

Fenelon

ALMIGHTY GOD, grant me THY grace to be faithful in action, and not anxious about success. My only concern is to do THY will, and to lose myself in THEE when engaged in duty. It is for THEE to give my weak efforts such fruits as THOU seest fit, none, if such be THY pleasure.

.: .: .:

Brother Lawrence

O LORD, the sense of THY love well-nigh overwhelms me. If it be THY will, bestow these many tokens of THY loving kindness on those who know THEE not, to draw them to THY service.

.: .: .:

Brother Lawrence

O Loving-Kindness so old and still so new, I have been too late in loving THEE.
O LORD, enlarge the chambers of my heart that I may find room for THY love.
Sustain me by THY Power, lest the fire of THY love consume me.

.: .: .:

Tersteegen

Draw near to my heart and inflame it. Touch my uncircumcised lips with a burning coal from THINE altar, that I may not speak of THINE ardent love in a cold or feeble manner.

.: .: .:

Tersteegen

Let THY love so warm our souls, O LORD, that we may gladly surrender ourselves with all we are and have unto THEE. Let THY love fall as fire from heaven upon the altar of our hearts, and teach us to guard it heedfully by continual devotion and quietness of mind.

Benjamin Jenks

O LORD, renew our souls and draw our hearts unto THYSELF, that our work may not be to us a burden but a delight, and give us such a mighty love for THEE as may sweeten all our obedience. O! let us not serve THEE with the spirit of bondage as slaves, but with the cheerfulness and gladness of children, delighting ourselves in THEE and rejoicing in THY work.

.·. .·. .·.

Blaise Palma

O ADMIRABLE WISDOM, that circlest all eternity, receivest into THYSELF all immensity, and drawest to THYSELF all infinity; from the inexhaustible fountain of THY light, shed some ray into my soul that I may more and more love whatever tends to THY glory and honour.

.·. .·. .·.

Melchior Ritter

O GOD, in THEE alone can our wearied souls have full satisfaction and rest, and in THY love is the highest joy. LORD, if we have THEE, we have enough.

.·. .·. .·.

John Wesley

O LORD, let us not live to be useless.

.·. .·. .·.

William Blake

Pour upon us THY Spirit of meekness and love. Annihilate selfhood in us. Be THOU all our life.

.·. .·. .·.

Newman

I am born to serve THEE, to be THINE, to be THY instrument. Let me be THY blind instrument. I ask not to see, ask not to know; I ask simply to be used.

**Collect
from the
18th
Century**

Grant us grace to rest from all sinful deeds and thoughts, to surrender ourselves wholly unto THEE, and keep our souls still before THEE like a still lake, so that the beams of THY grace may be mirrored therein, and may kindle in our hearts the glow of faith and love and prayer.

.:   .:   .:

Martineau

O GOD, Who hast commanded that no man should be idle, give us grace to employ all our talents and faculties in the service appointed for us; that, whatsoever our hand findeth to do, we may do it with our might. Cheerfully may we go on in the road which THOU hast marked out, not desiring too earnestly that it should be either more smooth or more wide; but daily seeking our way by THY light, may we trust ourselves and the issue of our journey, to THEE the Fountain of Joy, and sing songs of praise as we go along.

.:   .:   .:

Holmes

LORD, what am I, that with unceasing care THOU didst seek after me?

.:   .:   .:

Tagore

If THOU speakest not, I will fill my heart with THY silence and endure it. I will keep still and wait like the night with starry vigil and its head bent low with patience. The morning will surely come, the darkness will vanish, and THY voice pour down in golden streams, breaking through the sky.

Whittier

Dear GOD and FATHER of us all, forgive our faith in cruel lies; forgive the
blindness that denies; forgive THY creature when he takes, for the all-perfect Love
THOU art, some grim creation of his heart.

∴ ∴ ∴

**Charles
Kingsley**

Exalt us with THEE, O LORD, to know
the mystery of life, that we may use the
earthly as the appointed expression and
type of the heavenly, and by using to THY
glory the natural body may befit it to be
exalted to the use of the spiritual body.

∴ ∴ ∴

**Chr. G.
Rossetti**

O LORD, make us we implore THEE,
so to love THEE that THOU mayest be to
us a Fire of Love, purifying and not
destroying.

∴ ∴ ∴

**Chr. G.
Rossetti**

Love me in sinners and saints,
In each who needs or faints—
LORD, I will love THEE as I can
In every brother man.

∴ ∴ ∴

Tagore

Give me the strength lightly to bear
my joys and sorrows,
Give me the strength to make my love
fruitful in service.
Give me the strength to raise my mind
high above daily trifles,
And give me the strength to surrender
my strength to THY will with love.

R. Kipling

FATHER in heaven, who lovest all,
    O help THY children when they call;
That they may build from age to age,
    An undefiled heritage.

Teach us to bear THY yoke in youth,
    With steadiness and careful truth;
That, in our time, THY grace may give
    The truth whereby the nations live.

Teach us to rule ourselves alway
    Controlled and cleanly, night and
        day,
That we may bring, if need arise,
    No maimed or worthless sacrifice.

Teach us to look in all our ends
    On THEE for judge, and not our
        friends,
That we, with THEE, may walk uncowed
    By fear or favor of the crowd.

Teach us the strength that cannot seek,
    By deed or thought to hurt the weak;
That under THEE, we may possess
    THY strength, to succor man's
        distress.

Teach us delight in simple things,
    And mirth that has no bitter stings;
Forgiveness free of evil done,
    And love to all men 'neath the sun.

∴   ∴   ∴

**I. Wright
Beach**

Heavenly FATHER, THOU has healed me through the sweet restoring influence of divine love and I feel THY rich, new life now coursing through my entire body.

K. Tingley

O my DIVINITY! THOU dost blend with the earth and fashion for THYSELF temples of mighty Power.

O my DIVINITY! THOU livest in the heart-life of all things and dost radiate a Golden Light that shineth forever and doth illumine even the darkest corners of the earth.

O my DIVINITY! Blend THOU with me that from the corruptible I may become Incorruptible; that from imperfection I may become Perfection, that from darkness I may go forth in Light.

.·. .·. .·.

**N. H. D.
Golden
Words**

Let not my dreams of Things I hold most
    dear
Tie me to earth, but with a vision clear,
    Help me to build this day, dear LORD
    with THEE,
The things which last through all eternity.
    Attune my ears to hear THY message,
    LORD;
Inspire my lips to speak alone THY word.
    Veil THOU mine eyes from things I
    should not see,
Help me to leave my burdens all with
    THEE.

.·. .·. .·.

**Hindu
Prayer**

They who never ask anything but simply love, THOU in their heart abidest for ever, for this is THY very home.

.·. .·. .·.

**Hindu
Prayer**

Out of the unreal, lead me to the Real.
Out of the Darkness, lead me into the Light.
Out of Death, lead me to Deathlessness.

**Gorsedd
Prayer**

Grant, GOD, protection
And in protection, strength
And in strength, understanding
And in understanding, knowledge
And in knowledge, the knowledge of the
    just,
And in the knowledge of the just, the love
    of it,
And in the love of it, the love of all
    existences.
And in the love of all existences, the love
    of GOD,
GOD and all GOODNESS.

∴ ∴ ∴

**Earl
Brihtnoth**

O GOD, I thank THEE for all the joy
I have had in life.

∴ ∴ ∴

**Sister E. T.
Cawdry**

O GOD, THINE is the kingdom, the
power and the Glory, for ever and ever.
Amen.

∴ ∴ ∴

**Sister E. T.
Cawdry**

Let us go into the silence; O GOD,
our Heavenly FATHER, before THY altar
of love we come and in praise and adora-
tion we lift up our voices unto THEE. O
THOU great living light of the universe,
we THY children ask THEE to grant unto us
THY richest blessing and to remove all
shadow of doubt from our minds as regards
the life that awaiteth each one of us when
we too shall pass through the gates called
death. But we thank THEE, O GOD, that
the light of heaven has illumined our
Pathway and that THOU hast given unto
us this light that indeed is a living power
to sustain and to uphold us at all times.

John W. Chadwick

I do not pray because I would,
I pray because I must.
There's no beseeching in my prayer,
But thankfulness and trust.
And THOU wilt hear the thought I mean
And not the word I say,
Wilt hear the thanks between the words
That only seem to pray.

.: .: .:

Beatrice Colony

For health, prosperity and happiness
To THEE I pray,
But most of all a smile to greet
The newborn day.

.: .: .:

John Colet

Let not our sins be a cloud between
THEE and us.

.: .: .:

K. S. Guthrie

O HEAVENLY WISDOM, Who art the glorious fullness of the rays of Infinite Love and Righteousness, Piety and Justice, Tenderness and Stern Reproof, we supplicate for THY control. We would not willingly continue stumbling on in our old way. Our hearts are open to THY view; to the utmost are we willing to do Thy will. O that we might not be left unknowingly to leave the Narrow Way! Not because of the suffering which we willingly accept from THY dear Hand, but the withdrawing of THY dear Face. We will do our best; it shall be only for lack of Guidance if we fail to do THY Will. Amen.

**Walter
De Voe**

In divinest self surrender,
O my LORD, I come to THEE,
All my life to THEE I render;
I will THINE almoner be.

∴ ∴ ∴

**John
Keble**

Sun of my Soul, THOU SAVIOR DEAR!
It is not night if THOU be near.
O may no earth-born cloud arise
To hide THEE from THY servant's eyes.

∴ ∴ ∴

**Charles
How**

Most great and glorious GOD, be graciously pleased, I most humbly beseech THEE, to make the stream of my will perpetually to flow a cheerful and impetuous course, bearing down pleasure, interest, afflictions, death, and all other obstacles and impediments whatsoever, before it, till it plunge itself joyfully into the unfathomable ocean of THY DIVINE WILL.

∴ ∴ ∴

**Lady
Margery
Kempe
of Lynn**

LORD for THY great goodness, have mercy on my wickedness, as certainly I was never so wicked as THOU art good, nor never may be though I would; for THOU art so good that THOU mayest no better be.

∴ ∴ ∴

**Louis
Lisener**

Holy Spirit!
Give me a clear mind,
A pure heart,
A contrite spirit,
And a healthy body. Amen.

Richard Rolle

When so it liketh THEE, love speaks send THOU me; make mine heart all hot to be, burning in the love of THEE.

.: .: .:

Grenville Kleiser

If I can do some good today,
If I can serve along life's way,
If I can something helpful say,
    LORD, show me how!
If I can right a human wrong,
If I can help to make one strong,
If I can cheer with smile or song,
    LORD, show me how!
If I can aid one in distress,
If I can make a burden less,
If I can spread more happiness,
    LORD, show me how!
If I can do a kindly deed,
If I can help someone in need,
If I can sow a fruitful seed,
    LORD, show me how!
If I can feed a hungry heart,
If I can give a better start,
If I can fill a nobler part,
    LORD, show me how!

.: .: .:

Francis Rous

Let my love rest in nothing short of THEE, O GOD. Kindle and inflame and enlarge my love. Enlarge the arteries and conduit-pipes by which THOU, the Head and Fountain of Love, flowest in THY members, that being abundantly quickened and watered with the Spirit I may abundantly love THEE. Put THINE own image and beauty more and more on my soul.

**Veni
Cooper
Mathieson**

O great FATHER-MOTHER GOD.
THY eternal Life is my life.
THY infinite Wisdom guides me.
THY wondrous Intelligence illumines my
    mind.
THY glorious Substance feeds me.
THY perfect Health is revealed in me.
THY infinite Power upholds me.
THY almighty Strength is my support.
THY unchanging Love surrounds me.
THY eternal Truth has made me free.
THY perfect Peace broods over me.

.· .· .·

**Grace B.
Norris**

DIVINE LOVE, PRINCIPLE, GOD of
    love, I pray;
Guide me in the way of Truth
Tenderly, today.
Weed my heart of weariness, scatter
    every care.
Teach me how to know the truth:
Love is everywhere.

.· .· .·

F. W. Scott

THY glory alone, O GOD, be the end of
    all that we say;
Let it shine in every deed, let it kindle the
    prayers that I pray;
Let it burn in my innermost soul till the
    shadow of self pass away,
And the light of THY glory, O GOD, be
    unveiled in the dawning of day.

.· .· .·

Scupoli

Behold THY creature; do with me what
THOU wilt. I have nothing, my GOD,
that holds me back. I am THINE alone.

C. S. Tirpenting

ALMIGHTY LIFE! THOU FORCE that bides
    with all,
Awake my soul to see and use THY might,
And give me strength to heed THY daily
    call,
To walk with THEE in paths of truth and
    right.

Absolve me from all vain and useless
    thought
That clouds the vision of my daily task,
And help me labor in the field I ought
Till I can do for self the things I ask.

THOU art my harbor and my fortress too.
In THY strong arms support me on my
    way.

If THOU and I shall guard the things I do
I know I shall be safe by night and day.

∴   ∴   ∴

E. C. Wilson

Tomorrow
I am content to leave with him
Who gives today
For today the sun smiles
And the earth responds,
And a twinkling, singing sea
Forms lacy patterns on the sand.
O, GOD,
I am grateful
For this day!

∴   ∴   ∴

M. S. F.

Dear FATHER, we thank THEE for this
beautiful world.

**Henry
Vaughan**

THOU SUN of RIGHTEOUSNESS with
healing under THY wings, arise in my heart;
make THY light there to shine in darkness,
and a perfect day in the dead of night.

∴   ∴   ∴

**Walter
De Voe**

The Prayer of faith shall heal the sick.

∴   ∴   ∴

**Michael
Wood**

Within THY Heart, O HOLY ONE of
    GOD,
  Make us to rest;
Within THY still and changeless Heart,
    O LORD,
  Not on THY Breast.
THOU willest It shall tremble with our woes,
  Renouncing peace.
Feeling our joys that we may find our home,
  Where dreams shall cease.
Within THY Heart may we find earthly
    shows
  Close garner'd there by THEE;
The saints we honour'd, sinners whom we
    lov'd
  We in THY Heart shall see.
Within the still and changeless Light of
    Truth,
  The Wisdom from above,
We shall give honour where we lov'd and
    wept,
  And to the honour'd—love.

∴   ∴   ∴

Geibel

Strecke die Hand nur empor im Gebet,
GOTT fasst sie von oben,
  Und die Beruhrung durchstromt dich mit
geheiligter Kraft.

H.

FATHER—MOTHER—SON in ONE,
From our inmost hearts we plead
For power to love unselfishly,
For wisdom to perceive aright,
For courage to pursue a righteous course,
For determination of purpose, and
For will to act according to THY will.

∴ ∴ ∴

L. O. S.

Thy love provides for all
THY substance feeds all
THY Purity clothes all
THY life preserves all
Thanksgiving, honor, praise, and glory
    to THEE,
Evermore. Amen.

∴ ∴ ∴

Anonymous

Universal GOD,
Our Life,
Our Light,
Our Power!
THOU art in All beyond expression and
    beyond conception.
O Nature! THOU something from
    nothing
THOU Symbol of Wisdom!
In myself I am nothing, In THEE I am I.
I live in THEE! I, made of nothing!
Live THOU in me and bring me out of
    the region of self
Into the ETERNAL LIGHT.

∴ ∴ ∴

Emerson

Prayer is the contemplation of the facts
of Life from the highest Point of view.

Edward Rowland Sill

GOD be merciful to me, a fool.

∴   ∴   ∴

Belle-May

Prayer brings us into harmony with the highest in nature.

∴   ∴   ∴

Lamartine

Priere! O voix surnaturelle
Qui nous precipite a genoux;
Instinct du ciel qui nous rappelle
Que la patrie est loin de nous.

∴   ∴   ∴

Jehudah Halevi

Incline Thou mine heart
To do the service of Thy kingdom,
And my thought
Make pure for knowledge of Thy Godship.

∴   ∴   ∴

Solomon ibn Gabirol

In the flood of Thy love I have rapture
      eternal
And prayer is but an occasion for
      praise.

∴   ∴   ∴

Talmud

May it be Thy will, O God, that we return to Thee in perfect penitence, so that we may not be ashamed to meet our fathers in the life to come.

INDEX

(* Indicates Rosicrucian Authority)

EXPLANATORY

▽

THE ROSICRUCIAN ORDER

Anticipating questions which may be asked by the readers of this book, the publishers wish to announce that there is but one universal Rosicrucian Order existing in the world today, united in its various jurisdictions, and having one Supreme Council in accordance with the original plan of the ancient Rosicrucian manifestoes. The Rosicrucian Order is not a religious or sectarian society.

This international organization retains the ancient traditions, teachings, principles, and practical helpfulness of the Brotherhood as founded centuries ago. It is known as the *Ancient Mystical Order Rosae Crucis*, which name, for popular use, is abbreviated into AMORC. The headquarters for the Worldwide Jurisdiction of this Order is located at San Jose, California. Those interested in knowing more of the history and present-day helpful offerings of the Rosicrucian may have a free copy of the book entitled *The Mastery of Life* by sending a definite request to SCRIBE M.A.P., Rosicrucian Order AMORC, Rosicrucian Park, San Jose, California 95191, U.S.A.

THE ROSICRUCIAN LIBRARY

**VOL. I. ROSICRUCIAN QUESTIONS AND ANSWERS WITH
COMPLETE HISTORY OF THE ORDER**

The story of the Rosicrucian ideals, traditions, activities, and accomplishments is told interestingly in this book, and the scores of questions form a small encyclopedia of knowledge. Over 300 pages.

**VOL. II. ROSICRUCIAN PRINCIPLES FOR THE HOME
AND BUSINESS**

A very practical book dealing with the solution of health, financial, and business problems in the home and office.

VOL. III. THE MYSTICAL LIFE OF JESUS

A rare account of the Cosmic preparation, birth, secret studies, mission, crucifixion, and later life of the Great Master, from the records of the Essene and Rosicrucian brotherhoods. A book that is demanded in many lands as the most talked-about revelation of Jesus ever made.

VOL. IV. THE SECRET DOCTRINES OF JESUS

The secret teachings of the Master Jesus, for ages privately preserved in unknown archives, are herein brought to light. What are these teachings and why had men deleted them from the context of the Bible? The answer may be found in this beautiful book.

VOL. V. "UNTO THEE I GRANT . . ."

A strange book prepared from a secret manuscript found in a monastery of Tibet. It is filled with the most sublime teachings of the ancient Masters of the Far East. The book has had many editions. Attractive, with stiff cover.

VOL. VI. A THOUSAND YEARS OF YESTERDAYS

A beautiful story of reincarnation. This unusual book has been translated and sold in many languages and is universally endorsed.

**VOL. VII. SELF MASTERY AND FATE WITH THE
CYCLES OF LIFE**

A new and astounding system of determining your fortunate and unfortunate hours, weeks, months, and years throughout your life. No mathematics required. Better than any system of numerology or astrology.

VOL. VIII.   ROSICRUCIAN MANUAL

Most complete outline of the rules, regulations, and operation of lodges and student work of the Order, with many interesting articles, biographies, explanations, and complete Directory of Rosicrucian terms and words. Very completely illustrated. A necessity to every student who wishes to progress rapidly, and a guide to all seekers.

VOL. X.   BEHOLD THE SIGN

A book of ancient symbolism—the language that knows no boundary and has survived all ages. Mind speaking to mind across vast spaces of material deterioration. Each symbol clearly illustrated. An opportunity to learn the law of the Sword, the language of the Dragon, the message of the true Swastika cross. Impressively illustrated. A convenient gift size.

VOL. XI.   MANSIONS OF THE SOUL, THE COSMIC CONCEPTION

The complete doctrines of reincarnation explained. This book makes reincarnation easily understood.

VOL. XII.   LEMURIA—THE LOST CONTINENT OF THE PACIFIC

A fascinating revelation of the mystics and mysteries of a forgotten civilization. Read of the living descendants of these people, whose expansive nation now lies at the bottom of the Pacific. Beautifully bound, and contains many illustrations.

VOL. XIII.   THE TECHNIQUE OF THE MASTER

A guide to inner unfoldment! The newest and simplest explanation for attaining the state of Cosmic Consciousness. To those who have felt the throb of a vital power within, and whose inner vision has at times glimpsed infinite peace and happiness, this book is offered. It converts the intangible whispers of self into forceful actions that bring real joys and accomplishments in life. It is a masterful work on psychic unfoldment.

VOL. XIV.   THE SYMBOLIC PROPHECY OF THE GREAT PYRAMID

This book is a vivid portrayal of one of the greatest mysteries of the ages—The Great Pyramid. It is illustrated, well printed and beautifully bound.

VOL. XVII. MENTAL POISONING

Can envy, hate, and jealousy be projected through space from the mind of another and travel in poisonous rays to innocent victims? This book, one of the last written by Dr. H. Spencer Lewis, fearlessly deals with this psychological problem.

VOL. XVIII. GLANDS—THE MIRROR OF SELF

Now it is known that certain of the glands are governors which speed up or slow down the influx of cosmic energy into the body. This process of divine alchemy and how it works is explained in this book of startling facts.

VOL. XXII. THE SANCTUARY OF SELF

What could be more essential than the discovery and analysis of self, the composite of that consciousness which constitutes one's whole being? This book presents revealingly and in entirety the four phases of human living: The Mysteries, The Technique, The Pitfalls, and Attainment. Written authoritatively by Ralph M. Lewis, Imperator of the Rosicrucian Order (AMORC), this volume of 351 pages, carefully indexed, is of particular value as a text for teachers and students of metaphysics, including philosophy and psychology.

VOL. XXIII. SEPHER YEZIRAH

Among the list of the hundred best books in the world, one might easily include this simple volume, revealing the greatest authentic study of the secret Kabala. It has 61 pages with both Hebrew and English texts, photolithographed from the 1877 original edition of the translation by Dr. Isidor Kalisch. Paperback.

VOL. XXVI. THE CONSCIOUS INTERLUDE

Would you like to have your own mind look at itself in perspective? How many of the countless subjects which shape your life are inherited ideas? How many are actually yours? As you read through these pages, your mind will realize its own expanding consciousness. Indexed and illustrated.

VOL. XXVII. ESSAYS OF A MODERN MYSTIC

The writings of a true mystic philosopher constitute cosmic literature. The ideas they contain are born of *inner* experience—the self's contact with the cosmic intelligence residing within. Such writings, therefore, have the ring of conviction—of truth.

VOL. XXVIII. COSMIC MISSION FULFILLED

The life of Harvey Spencer Lewis, Imperator of the Ancient, Mystical Order Rosae Crucis, is a fascinating account of the struggle of a mystic-philosopher against forces of materialism. He was charged with the responsibility of rekindling the ancient flame of wisdom in the Western world.

VOL. XXIX. WHISPERINGS OF SELF

These are the interpretations of cosmic impulses received by a great mystic-philosopher, Ralph M. Lewis, who in this work writes under the pen name of Validivar. The aphorisms in this collection have appeared singly in copies of the *Rosicrucian Digest* over a period of forty years and comprise insights into all areas of human experience. A reader develops the habit of using a thought a day—there are more than two hundred to choose from. An attractive, hardcover book that makes a gift as well as a treasured possession of your own.

VOL. XXX. HERBALISM THROUGH THE AGES

The source of our first foods has a romantic and fascinating history. This book reveals man's discovery of natural foods, herbs, and their various uses through the centuries. Modern medical science uses many herbs whose real identity is obscured by technical medical terms. This book lists many of these herbs and tells their history and use.

VOL. XXXI. EGYPT'S ANCIENT HERITAGE

This book tells of the amazing similarity of Egyptian thought to modern religious, mystical, and philosophical doctrines, and how many of our customs and beliefs of today were influenced by these ancient people. It is truly an amazing revelation!

VOL. XXXII. YESTERDAY HAS MUCH TO TELL

Man's conquest of nature and his conflict with self, as written in the ruins of ancient civilizations, found in the sacred writings of temples and sanctuaries, and as portrayed in age-old tribal rites, are related to you by the author from his extensive travels and intimate experiences. The author was privileged because of his Rosicrucian affiliation to see and to learn that which is not ordinarily revealed. A hardbound book of 435 pages, including sixteen pages of photographs.

VOL. XXXIII. THE ETERNAL FRUITS OF KNOWLEDGE

Truths have a continuous value to man in inspiration and service. The ideas of philosophers and mystics of the past are realistic today. Such knowledge can serve us well now as it did earlier.

This volume deals with such subjects as the nature of the Absolute; body, mind and soul; good and evil; human and Universal Purpose, and other interesting topics. It is a well-printed paperbound book.

VOL. XXXIV. CARES THAT INFEST

We each have problems—but it is how we solve them that affects our individual development and our relationships with others. Learning comes from both our problems and from our solutions.

Realizing our weaknesses and basing our lives on a workable system of values will help each of us in our personal evolvement. This book discusses such specific problems as: worry, fear, and insomnia, and the development of a practical philosophy of life to alleviate the suffering caused by these difficulties.

This volume is attractively printed, bound, and stamped in gold.

VOL. XXXV. MENTAL ALCHEMY

Are we each responsible for the creation of our own surroundings? Perhaps not entirely—but by the proper mental attitude we can alter certain aspects of our lives, making them more compatible with our goals. It is easier to cope with a difficulty if we realize that, to some extent, we can transmute the problem to a workable solution through *mental alchemy*. The process is neither easy nor instantaneously effective.

This volume is attractively printed, bound, and stamped in gold.

VOL. XXXVI. MESSAGES FROM THE CELESTIAL SANCTUM

The real *unity* is Cosmic Unity. No human being is separated from the Cosmic, no matter where he lives or how different his life style may be. Each person is like a channel through which cosmically inspired intuitive impressions and guidance can flow. The *Celestial Sanctum* in general is the universe. No earthly sanctuary is more sacred than the multiple phenomena which occur in the great extensions of the Cosmic. There are no greater Laws than those which operate this phenomenon.

VOL. XXXVII. IN SEARCH OF REALITY

This Book Unites Metaphysics With Mysticism

Man is not just an isolated entity on Earth. He is also of a great world—the Cosmos. The forces that create galaxies and island universes also flow through man's being. The human body and its vital phenomenon—Life—are of the same spectrum of energy of which all creation consists. The universe is you because you are one of its myriad forms of existence. Stripping away the mystery of this Cosmic relationship increases the personal reality of the Self.

VOL. XXXVIII.   THROUGH THE MIND'S EYE

Truth Is What Is Real To Us. Knowledge, experience, is the material of which truth consists. But what is the *real, the true,* of what we know? With expanding consciousness and knowledge, truth changes. Truth therefore is ever in the *balance*—never the same. But in turning to important challenging subjects, the *Mind's Eye* can extract that which is the true and the real, for the *now.* The book, *Through The Mind's Eye,* calls to attention important topics for judgment by your mind's eye.

VOL. XXXIX.   MYSTICISM—THE ULTIMATE EXPERIENCE

An experience is more than just a sensation, a feeling. It is an *awareness,* or perception, with *meaning.* But there is *one* that transcends them all— the *mystical experience.* It serves every category of our being: it stimulates, it enlightens, it strengthens; it is the *Ultimate Experience.*

VOL. XL.   THE CONSCIENCE OF SCIENCE AND OTHER ESSAYS

A remarkable collection of fifty-four essays in the field of science and mysticism. Walter J. Albersheim's frank and outspoken manner will challenge readers to look again to their own inner light, as it were, to cope with the ponderous advances in modern technology.

VOL. XLI.   THE UNIVERSE OF NUMBERS

From antiquity, the strangest of systems attempting to reveal the universe has been that of numbers. This book goes back to the mystical meaning and inherent virtue of numbers. Paperback.

$$\triangledown \quad \triangledown \quad \triangledown$$

THE ROSICRUCIAN LIBRARY

Consists of a number of unique books which were described in the preceding six pages. They may be purchased from the

ROSICRUCIAN SUPPLY BUREAU
Rosicrucian Park, San Jose, California 95191, U.S.A.

For a complete, illustrated catalogue and price list
of the books listed herein, please write to the
Rosicrucian Supply Bureau